GET AFRAID

JOURNAL

TRY IT FOR THE STORY

Comfort Zone Challenges to Spark
Creativity and Inspire Adventure

JED STONEHAM

ISBN 978-1-7333819-0-1

Published by Jed Stoneham

Art and design by Jed Stoneham

Printed in the United States of America

IMPORTANT NOTE: This publication is written and sold with the understanding that the publisher is not providing psychological, financial, legal, or any other professional services. This book is offered strictly for informational purposes only. The publisher and author are providing information so you can have the knowledge and can choose, at your own risk, to act on that knowledge.

If expert counseling or advice is needed, the assistance of a health care professional should be sought. Readers are also urged to be aware of their health status and to consult with their medical practitioner before starting any health, diet, and/or exercise program.

Some challenges suggested in this journal may not be appropriate for unsupervised children.

www.getafraid.com

For Katie

In case of loss, please return to:

_____

_____

_____

HOW TO USE A

GET AFRAID
JOURNAL

Your instructions are to explore the unknown and report back.

You'll write, draw, and trash your way through a series of challenges designed to expand your comfort zone.

You may even have to act a little strange.

1. PICK A CHALLENGE

2. TRY IT FOR THE STORY

3. RECORD HOW IT WENT*

*However you want! Write, sketch, collect weird things, or even leave pages blank. Be as creative (or not) as you want to be.

YOU READY? THERE'S NO TURNING BACK NOW!

Well, I mean, you could go back and read the copyright page, but let's not get crazy.

#getafraid

ONE
MORE
THING
!!!!

———

Do whatever it takes to write or draw
comfortably. Even if it trashes the book.

Bend it, smash it, and
tear out pages.

———

IT'S YOUR JOURNAL
DON'T BE AFRAID TO MAKE IT YOURS

CHALLENGE TRACKER

Use this page to plan ahead and keep track of your progress.

Challenge	Page #	Complete
Start playing around with my new Get Afraid Journal	1	☒
		☐
		☐
		☐
		☐
		☐
		☐
		☐
		☐
		☐
		☐
		☐
		☐
		☐
		☐
		☐
		☐
		☐
		☐
		☐
		☐
		☐
		☐
		☐
		☐
		☐
		☐
		☐

Challenge (continued)	Page #	Complete
		☐
		☐
		☐
		☐
		☐
		☐
		☐
		☐
		☐
		☐
		☐
		☐
		☐
		☐
		☐
		☐
		☐
		☐
		☐
		☐
		☐
		☐
		☐
		☐
		☐
		☐
		☐
		☐
		☐
Finish the book!	100	☐

Start here, there, or wherever you want!

Just watch out for the bird. It's kind of a jerk.

"Who me? I just like being negative."

Ignore the bird. Let's begin.

WATCH THE
SCARIEST MOVIE
YOU CAN FIND FROM THE YEAR YOU WERE BORN

What did you watch? What was it about? Were you scared?

STEP OFF
DRY LAND

Go swimming, sailing, ice skating, or skiing. What did you try?

WRITE A VERY
BAD POEM

'Tis better to have poem'd and lost, than to never have poem'd at all.

GO FOR A
HIKE

Where did you go? What did you think about?

Make some art

THEN LEAVE THIS PAGE OUTSIDE FOR A MONTH

#getafraid

DON'T FORGET TO LEAVE YOUR ART OUTSIDE TO SEE WHAT HAPPENS

Don't litter! Make sure to post updates.

GET MAD

AND THROW A ROLL OF TOILET PAPER AT YOUR WALL SEVERAL TIMES

Was it strangely satisfying? What did you think about?

Pay Closer Attention
TO ONE OF YOUR SENSES TODAY
What did you choose? What new things did you notice?

14

"Hey it's me again! I just wanted to ask, what's the point?"

To have fun. Scribble it out and keep moving.

WHAT HAVE YOU ALWAYS WANTED TO TRY, BUT YOU'RE AFRAID?

Not big things like skydiving. Think of fears that are small and personal.

Try it for the story. What did you pick? How did it go?

DRAW SOMETHING
WICKED

Then trash this page.

17

DON'T FORGET TO **DESTROY** THIS PAGE AFTERWARD

18

Convert the Coin Jar into Cash

How much did you make? What do you want to use it for?

SPLURGE ON A FANCY
MASSAGE

How did it feel? Were you tense? Was it a waste of money?

20

LISTEN TO TOTALLY DIFFERENT
MUSIC

What did you try? What surprised you? Any new favorite songs?

21

get up an hour
EARLIER
tomorrow and get creative
Write or draw while your inner critic is still asleep.

22

Write to Your
FUTURE SELF

Tear it out and ask someone to hide it for you to find later.

wear a holiday outfit
when it's not even close to that holiday

What did you wear? Was it awkward? What did people say?

TRY THINGS

THAT START WITH THE FIRST LETTER OF YOUR BIRTH MONTH

What did you do? How hard was it to think of things?

"What's everyone going to say
when they find out?"

You tried that? I'd be too afraid.

WHAT DO YOU WANT TO TRY ALONE?

Museum? Theme park? Try it for the story. How did it go?

28

AVOID
reading & screens
AS MUCH AS YOU CAN TODAY

How did you occupy your time instead? Music, writing, crafts?

29

Visit a New Place
OF SPIRITUALITY OR CULTURE
Where did you go? What did you think? Would you go again?

TRY A TOTALLY DIFFERENT
HAIRSTYLE

Describe it. Do you love it or hate it? How did people react?

31

BUY YOUR FAVORITE CHILDHOOD
SNACK

What kind of memories did it stir up?

Write a Note

THEN TEAR IT OUT AND HIDE IT FOR SOMEONE

#getafraid

Go Find Nature
AND SOAK IT ALL IN

What kind of wildlife did you see? What did you hear?

Walk Barefoot

IN THE GRASS. WATCH YOUR STEP.

How was it? What's your earliest memory of being barefoot?

CONFESS

THEN TRASH THIS PAGE

What did you do?! Come clean, then destroy the evidence.

DON'T FORGET TO DESTROY THE EVIDENCE

38

"Not to be a downer, but aren't you too _____ to try that?"

Cover this with anything you can get your hands on.

WHAT DO YOU WANT TO TRY
BUT YOU THINK YOU'RE TOO OLD?

Try it for the story. How did it go? Did your age even matter?

40

skip FAST FOOD for a
WEEK

Was this easy or difficult? What did you eat instead?

BAKE SOMETHING
SUPER UGLY

What did you make? Green cookies? How did they taste?
Did you share with anyone?

SKETCH YOUR
DREAM HOME

Money and reality are no object. Why not a palace?
Flying house? Coral reef cabin?

GO TO A CITY
OR TOWN COUNCIL
MEETING

Or watch online. What was on the agenda? What did you learn?

44

GET ANGRY

Vent your frustrations over and over until you trash this page.

I'm upset I hate it when
Why doesn't anyone
It's always my fault
I'm mad at

DON'T FORGET TO
DESTROY
THIS PAGE AFTERWARD

TAKE A **COLD** SHOWER

How long did you last? What did it feel like?

GO TO THE MOVIES
ALONE

What did you see? Why? Was it awkward?

"It's a waste of time if it isn't perfect!"

Tear out this page and ruin it.

DON'T FORGET TO DESTROY THIS PAGE

WHAT WOULD YOU TRY IF YOU DIDN'T HAVE TO BE
THE BEST?

Fill the page. What sounds fun?

Podcasting

Drawing   Singing

Yoga   Making music   Volleyball

Filmmaking   Improv   Photography

Painting

Cosplay   Writing

Acting   Standup

Sculpture

What if you tried one?

51

VISIT A PLACE FROM YOUR
DISTANT PAST

Where did you go? Did it stir up good memories or bad ones?

Go to a Live
Performance
YOU WOULDN'T NORMALLY ATTEND

Concert, theater, sporting event? How was it?

Be Van Gogh
AND MAKE A SELF-PORTRAIT

Be Mona Lisa

AND LET SOMEONE SKETCH YOU

#getafraid

HOW DID IT FEEL TO DO A SELF-PORTRAIT COMPARED TO SOMEONE SKETCHING YOU?

What did you think of the results? Which did you like better?

BRING TREATS
FOR NO REASON

Class candy? Office donuts? What did people say?

TRAVEL
SOLO

Take half an hour or longer to explore. Where did you go? Why?

WHAT'S ONE OF YOUR MOST
EMBARRASSING MOMENTS?

Let it out and then trash this page.

DON'T FORGET TO **DESTROY** THIS PAGE AFTERWARD

"You really don't have time for this."

Maybe you could steal some time? I won't tell.

It's decision time. Should I...

_____ OR _____

Flip a coin to decide. Did you listen to the coin or your gut?

GET REALLY
SWEATY

Try exercise or spicy food. Any favorite sweaty memories?

Find an Object that Makes You Contemplate
EXISTENCE
A fossil? A globe? A meteorite? How did it make you feel?

GO OUT
DANCING

Where did you go? Who did you dance with? How fun was it?

List Five Things
THAT SCARE YOU

1. _____

2. _____

3. _____

4. _____

5. _____

NOW GO OUT AND TAKE A PICTURE
THAT REPRESENTS ONE!

#getafraid

66

WHAT DO YOU
REGRET?

Is there a way to learn from it? Can you let it go?

YOU MIGHT WANT TO DESTROY THIS PAGE AFTERWARD

create some
TERRIBLE ART
Then post a picture of it online.

HUG THREE
TREES

That was pretty weird. What kind of trees? Did anyone catch you?

REFLECT ON A TIME YOU
FAILED

What happened? How did you react? Would you try it again?

FEEL FREE TO
DESTROY
THIS PAGE AFTERWARD

FIND SOMETHING PAST ITS EXPIRATION DATE
AND SKETCH IT WEARING A TOP HAT

What was the expiration date? _____

GET CAUGHT
STRUTTING IN PUBLIC
How did it feel? Embarrassing? Did anyone join in?

"You can put it off again. No rush!"

Scratch this out ASAP!

WHAT'S SOMETHING YOU'VE BEEN
AVOIDING?

Fill the page. What sounds most rewarding?

Calling back

Exercising Making changes

Signing up. Thanking Booking a trip

Finishing A tough conversation

Forgiving

Commitment Self-care

Sleep

Applying Decluttering

Taking time off

What if you finally did it?

76

START WRITING A
LETTER

Who is it for? Do you want to send it to them?

TRY TO MAKE A STRANGER
LAUGH

How many times did you fail? Did you succeed?

VISIT A
CEMETERY

Where did you pay your respects? What did you think about?

GO OUT TO EAT
ALONE

Don't look at your phone or read. How did it go?

Write Down

YOUR DEEPEST INSECURITIES

Then trash this page.

DON'T FORGET TO DESTROY THIS PAGE AFTERWARD

COMPLIMENT THREE
STRANGERS

What did you say? How did they react? Was it uncomfortable?

ASK A FRIEND TO WRITE THREE CHALLENGES FOR YOU

_____

_____

_____

Try one! How did it go? Why that one? Want to try the others?

#getafraid

"Hey what's up? You're still doing this book?
I don't think anyone's ever finished it."

I believe in you.

SIGN UP FOR A
CLASS

What did you pick? How was the first class? Were you nervous?

Express Your Mood

REVEAL WHAT KEEPS YOU UP
AT NIGHT

Express your worries and get them out of your head.

Ask Strangers

IF YOU CAN TAKE THEIR PHOTO

What did they say? Were you rejected? How did you feel?

WHERE DO YOU SEE YOURSELF IN
100 YEARS?

What do you want to be remembered for? What's your legacy?

WHAT HAVE YOU ALWAYS WANTED TO TRY, BUT YOU'RE AFRAID?

Not big things like skydiving. Think of fears that are small and personal.

Try it for the story. How did it go?

#getafraid

(The publisher and author are providing information so you can have the knowledge and can choose, at your own risk, to act on that knowledge.)

WALK 10K STEPS
AND COUNT THEM MANUALLY

Where did you go? How far, or high, did you get? Did you cheat?

CATCH A SUNRISE AND SUNSET
ON THE SAME DAY

The early bird gets the worm for breakfast and dessert.
Which was better? Where did you go?

FINAL CHALLENGE

Flip back and read through
your journal entries!

What have you learned?
How have you grown?
What's next?

---

*Use the following pages to
record your thoughts.*

#getafraid

#getafraid

#getafraid

YOU'VE REACHED
THE END
Congratulations!

Feel free to jump back and try any challenges you skipped!

Facing fears can feel amazing. You may notice a boost in confidence and a sense of satisfaction after trying to expand your comfort zone.

You'll always have new fears, but you can always:

GET AFRAID
AND TRY IT FOR THE STORY

Thanks for playing!

Discover your next adventure at
www.getafraid.com

"Congrats! We did it! I'm gonna take
all the credit though."

Acknowledgments

I owe a huge thank you to my wonderful editor Molly McCowan, whose patient guidance and enthusiastic encouragement helped shape this work. Thanks to Adam Rosen for introducing us.

Special thanks to my partner Katie Honeman for her patience as I rambled on about this book every day, and for her valuable suggestions along the way.

I also wish to thank Kimmie Companik-Warner for teaching me to say "yes and," Julie Williams for daring me to make a stranger laugh, and Drew Ackerman for his timely wisdom.

I am particularly grateful for the valuable feedback of my playtesters — Kimmie, Jeff, Sarah, and Rebecca.

Finally, I wish to thank my family and friends for their never-ending support and helpful advice.

About the Author

Jed Stoneham is a designer and writer. In 2015, he started doing things he was afraid of for the podcast *Man Afraid of Everything*, recording every single worry along the way. He started small and worked his way up to improv comedy. Jed's a graduate of Bradley University and the Comedy Writing and Beginning Improv program at Second City Chicago. He currently resides in Chicago. This is his first book.

For email updates on the author, visit www.getafraid.com.